IMAGES
of America

THE STATUE
OF LIBERTY

LIBERTY ENLIGHTENING THE WORLD. The Statue of Liberty has been an abiding symbol of the American people for more than 100 years. (National Park Service.)

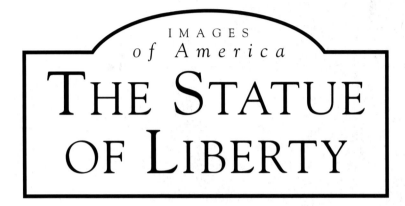

IMAGES
of America
THE STATUE
OF LIBERTY

Barry Moreno

ARCADIA

Published by Arcadia Publishing
Charleston SC, Chicago IL, Portsmouth NH, San Francisco CA

Printed in Great Britain

Library of Congress Catalog Card Number: 2004109814

For all general information contact Arcadia Publishing at:
Telephone 843-853-2070
Fax 843-853-0044
E-mail sales@arcadiapublishing.com
For customer service and orders:
Toll-Free 1-888-313-2665

Visit us on the internet at http://www.arcadiapublishing.com

Dedicated to my colleague Jeffrey S. Dosik.

CONTENTS

Introduction   7

1.   Libertas   9

2.   The Sculpture Takes Form   23

3.   The Pedestal   39

4.   To America   53

5.   The Colossus of New York   65

6.   The Golden Jubilee   87

7.   America's Great Lady   97

8.   Fortress of Freedom   117

Index   127

INTRODUCTION

The *Images of America* series would be quite incomplete without a book on the Statue of Liberty, for this monument is internationally recognized as the single most potent symbol of the American spirit of freedom and democracy. But unlike America's many other symbols, such as the Stars and Stripes, the bald eagle, or Uncle Sam, Liberty was not a homegrown icon: the colossal sculpture was given to the United States as an anniversary present from the country's oldest ally, France. Thus the story of Liberty's origins and birth takes us to Paris, the city of light, in the year 1865, where the statue's creator, Edouard de Laboulaye, was employed as a professor of legal history at one of the city's greatest schools, the Collège de France. To a group of his political and intellectual friends, he suggested that the time had come for Frenchmen to remind the Americans of the special relationship that their respective nations had towards each other, a relationship that involved the American War of Independence, the Founding Fathers, and the Marquis de Lafayette. In addition, he wished to praise the United States as the repository of liberty in a world where most nations, including France, were still ruled by undemocratic governments.

By 1871, following the collapse of authoritarian rule in France, Laboulaye was joined by the sculptor Frederic-Auguste Bartholdi in this scheme. The idea was to sculpt a monumental statue of Liberty and present it as a gift to the American people in honor of their first 100 years of independence. The form the statue would take was a simple one for Laboulaye and Bartholdi to select: it would simply be Libertas, the classical goddess of freedom, who was already a recognized symbol of the French Republic and had made her appearance for many years previously on French and American coinage. The goddess was an old one, dating back to ancient Rome, where she had been worshipped by the religious men and women of antiquity who had cherished freedom from slavery. The choice of a goddess to personify a nation's spirit was part of the classical heritage of European civilization, and it demonstrated the efficacy of the beautiful forms and ideas of Roman art and philosophy in representing the genius of a modern nation. Great Britain's powerful symbol Britannia grew out of this same tradition.

This book tells the long story of the Statue of Liberty: the story of her creators Laboulaye and Bartholdi and their principal helpers, Eugène Viollet-le-Duc and Gustave Eiffel in Paris and William Evarts and Richard Hunt in New York; the story of her unveiling in 1886; and the story of her service to the people of the United States unto this very day. The chapters lead the reader through Liberty's many roles. She has been a symbol of Franco-American friendship, of American independence, and of freedom from slavery and tyranny. She has been the "mother of exiles" to immigrants and refugees. And she remains the ultimate patriotic symbol of the country, a universal symbol of freedom to all nations and all peoples.

—Barry Moreno
Staten Island
August 2004

One

LIBERTAS

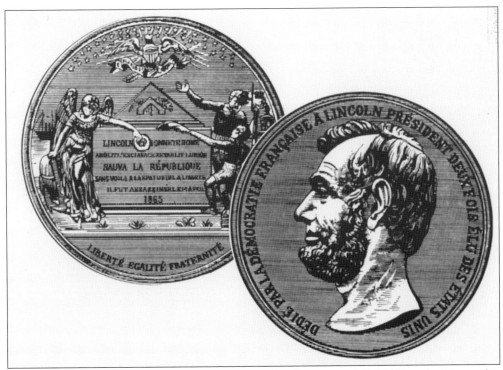

THE FRANCO-SWISS LINCOLN MEDAL. Thanks to the donations of 40,000 French citizens, this gold medal was cast in Switzerland in 1865 as a memorial tribute to slain president Abraham Lincoln. It pays homage to Lincoln as an honest man who "abolished slavery, re-established the Union and saved the republic, without veiling the statue of liberty." The coin was presented to the president's widow, Mary Lincoln. After her death, their son, Robert Lincoln, donated it to the Library of Congress. (National Park Service.)

EDOUARD RENE LEFEBVRE DE LABOULAYE. In 1865, Edouard de Laboulaye (1811–1883) dreamed up the idea of presenting a monumental gift to the United States in commemoration of its upcoming centenary of independence. At the time, Laboulaye was France's leading expert on the United States and was also a great admirer of the country. He advocated democratic government in France at a time when the country was under the tight reins of Emperor Napoleon III. Laboulaye was a professor of constitutional law and history at the Collège de France in Paris, the city of his birth. (National Park Service.)

A BUST OF EDOUARD DE LABOULAYE. In 1866, the young sculptor Auguste Bartholdi sculpted this bust of Professor Laboulaye. It was in the previous year that the two men had become acquainted and Laboulaye had shared his idea of building a monument for America. But in view of Napoleon's monarchy, Laboulaye's idea seemed rather dangerous, and for a time it remained merely a dream. (National Park Service.)

A Coin of Libertas, Goddess of Liberty. For decades, the Roman goddess Libertas has been an official symbol of each French Republic (including the present Fifth Republic). Laboulaye admired the symbol because he regarded it as a less radical one than Marianne, the symbol of the French revolutionaries. Laboulaye had served under the short-lived Second Republic (1848–1852), and when it perished, Libertas was dispensed with as well. It is small wonder that when he had the idea to build a monument for America, he decided that it would take the form of this goddess.

LIBERTY STANDING. Here the Roman goddess Libertas holds the Phrygian bonnet of a freed slave in her right hand and her scepter in her left hand. These were only two of her sacred attributes. Libertas also appeared on French, U.S., and Mexican coins.

THE REVERSE OF THE LIBERTAS COIN. This side of the coin bears the signature of Brutus, who issued it to proclaim that he was a defender of liberty.

13

FREDERIC-AUGUSTE BARTHOLDI. The young sculptor Auguste Bartholdi (1834–1904) was a native of Alsace, a province in eastern France. He lived most of his life in Paris, however, where he achieved fame as a sculptor. He was noted for his large-scale political statuary done in a traditional style. His greatest works are *Liberty Enlightening the World* and *Lion of Belfort.* (National Park Service.)

PROCLAIM LIBERTY THROUGH-OUT ALL THE LAND UNTO ALL THE INHABITANTS THEREOF.

Leviticus, XXV, 10.

Inscribed on the Liberty Bell, Independence Hall, Philadelphia, Pa. The original source of the quotation is Leviticus, third book of the Old Testament.

THE LIBERTY BELL. This inscription from Colonial times symbolizes America's long admiration for liberty. Edouard de Laboulaye carefully studied the advance of liberty and political democracy in the United States from its earliest times. His own writings were influenced by the ideas of Benjamin Franklin, Horace Mann, and William Ellery Channing. (F. Nigro, National Park Service, 1952.)

EMPEROR NAPOLEON III. Edouard de Laboulaye strongly objected to the authoritarian rule of Emperor Napoleon III, but he feared the emperor's secret police. He wanted France to rid itself of this form of government and become a constitutional democracy like the United States. His idea of giving a statue of Liberty to the Americans was one way of underlining the importance of democracy against tyranny. Napoleon's rule came to an end early in the Franco-Prussian War (1870–1871).

THE COLOSSUS OF RHODES.
Auguste Bartholdi studied the colossal statuary of the ancient Greeks and Egyptians with avidity. The celebrated statue of the sun god, Helios (known popularly as the "Colossus of Rhodes"), influenced Bartholdi's bold plans for the statue of Libertas. Like Helios, Libertas would stand at the entrance to a harbor, would hold aloft a lamp, and would have upon her head a *nimbus* (in the form of a spiked halo). But Helios stood only 110 feet high, while Libertas was to rise to a height of 151 feet 1 inch. (National Park Service.)

EGYPT CARRYING THE LIGHT TO ASIA. Auguste Bartholdi's first important venture into modeling a great monument in the tradition of the Colossus of Rhodes was called *Egypt Carrying the Light to Asia.* In 1867, the sculptor proposed building this colossus for the reigning Egyptian khedive, Isma'il Pasha. Taking the form of a veiled Egyptian peasant woman, the statue was to stand 86 feet high, and its pedestal was to rise to a height of 48 feet. Fearing it would incur too great an expense, Isma'il Pasha rejected the offer in 1869. (U.S. Army Signal Corps, James W. Todd, Colmar, France, 1945.)

THE EGYPTIAN MODELS. These clay models (called *maquettes* in French) of *Egypt Carrying the Light to Asia* show the different poses that the artist was toying with. The variations of stance, movement, headdress, and lantern are particularly evident. (U.S. Army Signal Corps, James W. Todd, Colmar, France, 1945.)

A Movement of a Different Sort.
In the clay model at left, Egypt is quite
heavily draped in elegant flowing
robes and bears aloft a stylized lantern,
while her left hand clutches a portion
of her robe. Below, a more complete
conception of the monument is
shown, as Egypt stands on a quite
magnificent pedestal and bears aloft an
enormous lantern to light the entrance
to the Suez Canal, where she was to
stand. The pedestal is reminiscent of
the ancient lighthouse of Alexandria,
which to its Greek creators was
known as the *pharos*. (U.S. Army
Signal Corps, James W. Todd, Colmar,
France, 1945.)

LIBERTY: THE BIRTH OF AN ICON.
Disappointed by the Egyptian khedive's refusal to engage him to sculpt the Suez Canal statue, Bartholdi decided to accept Laboulaye's more political project. From 1870 to 1871, Bartholdi made several clay models of the goddess of Liberty. The model pictured at right shows Liberty holding the torch in her right hand, whilst in her left she holds a bit of a broken chain.

The sculptured figure below conforms to Edouard de Laboulaye's image for Liberty. In her right hand she bears aloft the torch, in her left hand she holds the tablet signifying constitutional law, upon her head is a diadem, and at her feet is the broken shackle and chain of oppression. Her Roman drapery (*stola* and *palla*) is classical in every fold. (U.S. Army Signal Corps, James W. Todd, Colmar, France, 1945.)

BARTHOLDI'S CLAY MODELS. This image shows the various clay models or *maquettes* for several of Auguste Bartholdi's artistic projects, including *Liberty Enlightening the World* and *Egypt Carrying the Light to Asia*. They are a part of the collection of the Bartholdi Museum in Colmar, France. (National Park Service.)

BARTHOLDI'S VISION OF NEW YORK. In 1871, the sculptor sailed to the United States and made this sketch of New York Harbor and the surrounding metropolitan area. He was enthusiastic on entering the bay, for he spotted a small island that his artistic instinct whispered to him would be the perfect home for the Statue of Liberty. The site of his inspiration, Bedloe's Island, then housed an active army base known as Fort Wood. (National Park Service.)

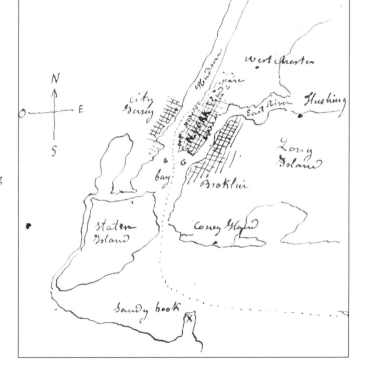

BARTHOLDI THE FREEMASON.
In 1875, Auguste Bartholdi became a freemason and was initiated into the Alsace-Lorraine lodge in Paris. The sculptor's Masonic knowledge probably strengthened his commitment to the Statue of Liberty as a symbol of democratic enlightenment.

THE MARQUIS DE LAFAYETTE. With the consent of King Louis XVI, the Marquis de Lafayette played a decisive role in U.S. history by helping the American colonies to win their independence from Great Britain. To achieve this end, the marquis worked closely with Gen. George Washington. Pictured here is Auguste Bartholdi's statue of the Marquis de Lafayette that stands in New York's Union Square. It was unveiled in 1876. (National Park Service.)

21

Liberty Enlightening the World on Bedloe's Island. Auguste Bartholdi executed this watercolor painting of the Statue of Liberty in 1875 and named it *La statue en place sur Bedloe's Island*. The painting gave Edouard de Laboulaye and his circle of intimates a clearer notion of how the monument would look positioned on the little isle in New York Harbor. (National Park Service.)

Gen. William T. Sherman. From 1876 to 1877, Bartholdi made his second trip to the United States. On this occasion, the New York friends of Laboulaye set up the American Committee to promote the project. Due to the committee's influence, Congress voted in 1877 to accept the statue, and Pres. Rutherford B. Hayes soon authorized General Sherman to select a site for the projected monument. Sherman granted Bartholdi's wish for Bedloe's Island. (National Park Service.)

Two

THE SCULPTURE
TAKES FORM

THE BANQUET OF LIBERTY. This was the Franco-American Union's kickoff fund-raising gala for the Statue of Liberty. The dazzling affair was hosted by Edouard de Laboulaye and took place at the elegant Hotel du Louvre on November 6, 1875. At the banquet, Laboulaye unveiled the final model for the statue and his initial plans for raising money to complete it. (*Le Journal Illustré*, Paris, 21 November 1875.)

THE FRANCO-AMERICAN UNION FUND-RAISING CAMPAIGN. Shown here is a subscription form to be filled in by donors to the Statue of Liberty project. Edouard de Laboulaye had founded the union in 1875 and served as its president. He created the French Committee in Paris and authorized the setting up of American committees in the United States. Aside from Laboulaye and Bartholdi, members of the French Committee included Henri Martin, C. F. Dietz-Monnin, Count Oscar de Lafayette, Jules de Lasteyrie, Paul de Rémusat, Count Hippolyte de Tocqueville, William Waddington, Cornélis de Witt, Jean Macé, Count Sérurier, Louis Wolowski, Louis-Laurent Simonin, Victor Borie, Eugène Viollet-le-Duc, Jean-Francois Bozérian, Honoré Monduit, and Emile Gaget.

A Musical Triumph at the Paris Opera. In April 1876, Laboulaye and his Franco-American Union organized this splendid fundraiser at the Paris Opera. There, Laboulaye delivered an important address concerning the Liberty project. He was followed by a matchless "solemnity of music," which concluded with Charles Gounod's musical tribute, *La Liberte éclairant le monde.*

THÉATRE NATIONAL DE L'OPÉRA

MARDI 25 AVRIL 1876, à Huit heures et demie du soir

SOLENNITÉ MUSICALE

ORGANISÉE PAR LE COMITÉ

DE L'UNION FRANCO-AMÉRICAINE

POUR L'ÉRECTION D'UN MONUMENT COMMÉMORATIF À L'OCCASION DU

CENTENAIRE DE L'INDÉPENDANCE DES ETATS-UNIS

Membres d'honneur :

M. WASHBURNE, Ministre plénipotentiaire des États-Unis à Paris.
M. AM. BARTHOLDI, Ministre plénipotentiaire de France à Washington.
Mis DE NOAILLES, Ambassadeur de France à Rome. Mis DE ROCHAMBEAU.
M. W. FORNEY, Commissaire général en Europe de l'Exposition des États-Unis.
M. ÉDOUARD LABOULAYE, Président du Comité, Directeur.
MM. HENRI MARTIN et DIETZ-MONIN, Vice-Présidents.
MM. Oscar de LAFAYETTE, Jules de LASTEYRIE, Paul de RÉMUSAT, Comte de TOCQUEVILLE,
WADDINGTON, CORNÉLIS DE WITT, Jean MACÉ, Comte SERRURIER
L. SIMONIN, V. BORIE, A. BARTHOLDI, A. GAUBERT, DE LAGORSSE.

COMMISSION MUSICALE ORPHÉONIQUE

Docteur E. SAILLY, Président

Membres: MM. ARTAUD, E. DETOUCHE, E. D'INGRANDE, CH. LEFÈVRE, H.-A. SIMON, G. VÉLY

CONFÉRENCE SUR LES ÉTATS-UNIS ET LA FRANCE

Par M. ÉDOUARD LABOULAYE, de l'Institut

Solennité avec le concours de

Mlle ROSINE BLOCH   Mlle ROUSSEIL   M. CARON

LES ARTISTES DE L'ORCHESTRE DE L'OPÉRA

Et les SOCIÉTÉS ORPHÉONIQUES du département de la Seine.

Sociétés cho siles de deo vien expérience, 600 Exécutans.

PREMIÈRE PARTIE

1. Ouverture de la Muette de Portici....... AUBER.
   Exécutée par l'Orchestre de l'Opéra.
2. Discours-conférence par M. E. LABOULAYE.
3. Les Rameaux [avec orchestre]........... FAURE.
   Chantés par M. CARON.
4. Les Martyrs aux Arènes............. L. VERDIER.
   Choeur chanté par toutes les Sociétés,
   sous la direction de l'auteur.

5. Ave Maria,.................... GOUNOD.
   Avec accompagnement de Violon, Orgue
   et Harpe par MM. Garcin, Hector, Sa-
   homan et C. Premier.
   t hauté par Mlle ROSINE BLOCH.
6. Ap te rent das.,.............. R. MAX.
   Poésie
   Dite par Mlle ROUSSEIL.

DEUXIÈME PARTIE

1. Ouverture de Guillaume Tell .... ROSSINI.
   Exécutée par l'orchestre de l'Opéra.
2. Caroline d'Avant de zémit-m-z,..... SONNINI.
   chantée par Mlle R. BLOCH (orchestre)
3. Sur les Remparts.................. MARTINI.
   Choeur chanté par toutes les Sociétés,
   sous la direction de l'auteur.
4. Le Soldat.......................
   Poésie de M. Paul DESCOLRSE, mise en
   musique et orchestré par,.......... A. COTTIN.
   Chanté par M. CARON.

5. La Liberté éclairant le Monde.......
   Hymne à 4 voix d'hommes
   Paroles d'Emma Gétan, musique de CH. GOUNOD
   Chantée par toutes les Sociétés chorales;
   accompagnée par l'Orchestre de l'Opéra.
   [Première audition, 700 choristers].
   Joue le d.rénou de M. CH. GOUNOD.
6. Hail C-lumbia,...............
   Air national américain
   Orchestré par M. Victor Poise.
   Exécuté par l'Orchestre de l'Opéra.

L'ORGUE SORT DES ATELIERS DE LA MAISON ALEXANDRE

LE PRIX DES PLACES N'EST PAS AUGMENTÉ. — Les Dames sont admises à l'Orchestre.

Pour cette solennité, les croiers de l'abonnement, Les Loges de Rez-de-Chaussée, y seclet roug, et les index Leg v i r
Face, seli menté à ce deponsibles du palluc.

LE BUREAU DE LOCATION EST OUVERT TOUS LES JOURS, DES AUREE, DE 10 HEURES À ½ HEURES.

Paris. — Typ. M-nant père et fils, rue Amery, 9..

The Copper King. The French donations flowing to the Statue of Liberty were not only in the form of money. Learning that engineer Eugène Viollet-le-Duc recommended that the statue be built of copper, industrialist Pierre-Eugène Secretan donated 128,000 pounds of the metal to the Franco-American Union. The total amount of copper used for the statue was 200,000 pounds. The metal was an exceptionally pure grade and came from a Franco-Belgian mine in Vigsnes, Karmoy, Norway. Auguste Bartholdi sculpted this bust of his friend Pierre Secretan. (Christian Kempf, Bartholdi Museum, Colmar, France.)

EUGÈNE-EMMANUEL VIOLLET-LE-DUC. Eugène Viollet-le-Duc (1814–1879) was one of the 19th century's greatest engineers and architects. He attained distinction as a restorer of historic buildings and as an expert on medieval fortifications. In 1875, Auguste Bartholdi, who had studied architecture under Viollet-le-Duc, persuaded his old professor to serve as the engineer of the Statue of Liberty project. Viollet-le-Duc recommended that the colossal statue be built of copper and sculptured using the *repoussé* technique. These suggestions were adopted and proved quite effective. The engineer also recommended that the hollow copper statue be filled with sand so that it would not collapse. However, Viollet-le-Duc died suddenly while on a trip to Switzerland in 1879, and this last suggestion was abandoned. He was succeeded by Gustave Eiffel, who created a different internal system for the monument. Politically, Viollet-le-Duc was an anti-royalist and a radical republican.

HONORÉ MONDUIT. Monduit operated the Paris foundry where the Statue of Liberty was constructed. Eugène Viollet-le-Duc recommended Monduit's foundry as the best construction firm to handle the contract. Monduit supervised the building of the right hand, torch, and flame of the statue. He retired from the business shortly after having finished this contract. He was succeeded by his younger partners, Emile Gaget and J. G. Gauthier, who built the rest of the statue.

GAGET, GAUTHIER ET COMPAGNIE. Pictured here is the commercial poster of the metal foundry headed by Emile Gaget and J. B. Gauthier following Honoré Monduit's retirement. Dating from 1880, the poster highlights the firm's major work contracts, including its construction of the Statue of Liberty, which was still in progress.

INSIDE THE GAGET AND GAUTHIER FOUNDRY. This photograph shows the wooden molds that were used to sculpt the statue's copper sheets into her shape. Sections of the statue were first fashioned in plaster. Carpenters then built wooden forms that duplicated the plaster shape. After that, thin sheets of heated copper were made ready for hammering into shape (*repoussé*) on the wooden forms. Some of the stages of the *repoussé* sculpturing technique can be seen in this image. (The New York Public Library.)

A PORTRAIT OF AUGUSTE BARTHOLDI. Auguste Bartholdi used his genius for organizing and commanding the workers so as to ensure that no blunders or infelicities were introduced in the fabrication of the magnificent monument. Tirelessly, he prodded them on, corrected them, and guided them. (National Park Service.)

THE CONSTRUCTION OF THE TORCH AND FLAME, 1876. Inside the Gaget and Gauthier foundry's special workshop, Liberty's magnificent torch, flame, and upper right hand near completion.

A PUBLIC DISPLAY OF THE TORCH AND FLAME, 1876. The Statue of Liberty's completed torch and flame were shipped to the United States in September 1876 and displayed at the U.S. Centennial Exhibition in Philadelphia. The awesome construction created a sensation, for Americans at last had an idea of the size of the monument that the French had in store for them. (National Park Service.)

CHARLOTTE BARTHOLDI, 1855.
Auguste Bartholdi's mother, Charlotte Bartholdi (1801–1891), provided the artist with every comfort so that he could achieve his goals as a sculptor. In gratitude, Bartholdi liked to say that she had been the model for the Statue of Liberty. (National Park Service.)

MOLDING THE HEAD OF LIBERTY.
The head and shoulders of the goddess of Liberty were molded during the first half of 1878. (National Park Service.)

THE HEAD OF LIBERTY ON DISPLAY, 1878. The gigantic head and shoulders of Liberty caused a sensation when they were put on display at the Paris Universal Exposition in July 1878. The bust stood in the Champs de Mars, and tourists paid a small fee to go inside and climb up to the crown. (National Park Service.)

THE LIBERTY DIORAMA. In 1877, Bartholdi created a diorama exhibit to raise funds for the Statue of Liberty project. He painted scenes of New York Harbor and the Statue of Liberty standing in place on Bedloe's Island. The paintings created the illusion of riding a steamboat in the city's wondrous harbor. The diorama was first exhibited at the Palais de l'Industrie and was then shown at the Jardin de Tuileries. It raised a large amount of money for the Franco-American Union. Bartholdi dismantled the exhibit in 1879.

THE CONSTRUCTION OF THE PLASTER ARMS, UPPER TORSO, AND TABLET. Before the statue could be fashioned into copper, full-size sections had to be made out of plaster. Pictured here are plasterers and other craftsmen busy at their tasks. (National Park Service.)

ALEXANDRE-GUSTAVE EIFFEL. In 1879, Gustave Eiffel (1832–1923) succeeded Eugène Viollet-le-Duc as the engineer for the project. Eiffel accepted his predecessor's sculpturing specifications; his task was instead to create an internal structural system that would hold the metal statue in place. This he achieved by designing a complicated skin-support and attachment system of iron armature bars, a 92-foot-high, powerfully trussed tower (pylon), and a skeletal framework bolted to the pylon and the skin. (National Park Service.)

GOODRIDGE'S PLAN FOR THE ERECTION OF BARTHOLDI'S STATUE.

Fig. 2.—PLAN OF BRACING AND TUBE.

Fig. 3.—INTERIOR BRACING AND FRAME.

Fig. 4.—MODE OF SETTING UP THE STATUE, GIVING INTERIOR TUBE, AND BRACING.

Fig. 5. THE STATUE AND PEDESTAL NEARLY COMPLETE

Fig. 6. THE STATUE SET UP COMPLETE AND READY FOR ELEVATION.

GOODRIDGE'S PLAN FOR THE ERECTION OF THE STATUE OF LIBERTY AND ITS PEDESTAL IN NEW YORK HARBOR.

GOODRIDGE'S ALTERNATIVE STRUCTURE FOR LIBERTY. The journal *Scientific American* published this article about the construction of the Statue of Liberty in May 1883. This page of the story focuses on John C. Goodridge's alternative plan for holding the statue in place. His design is noticeably different from Gustave Eiffel's in that it was at once heavier and less elegant. (National Park Service.)

THE RIVET-DRIVING CEREMONY IN PARIS, 1881. On October 24, 1881, Levi Parsons Morton, the American ambassador to France, drove in the first rivet for the assembly of the Statue of Liberty. This marked the stage that everyone was waiting for: putting the pieces of the goddess together on her newly designed framework of iron. (National Park Service.)

THE PYLON AND FRAMEWORK OF THE STATUE OF THE LIBERTY. This photograph was taken by Pierre Petit in November 1881 and shows the completion of the first stage of the assembly of the Statue of Liberty. (National Park Service.)

THE CONSTRUCTION TO THE LEVEL OF THE HIPS. At this level, the colossal goddess gradually begins to make her epiphany. Her other accoutrements are ready when required. Her head and torch rest on the ground. The work was tedious and slow, and even the scaffold was incomplete at this stage of the work. (National Park Service.)

THE MOUNTING OF THE HEAD AND ARM. This 1883 photograph shows the steady growth of the statue and the greatest height that the scaffold achieved. One of the more difficult tasks was attaching the arm. The statue's builders, Gaget and Gauthier, positioned the arm too close to the head. This blunder created problems in later years. (National Park Service.)

ENTERING LIBERTY THROUGH HER FOOT. Auguste Bartholdi took this photograph near the entrance of the Statue of Liberty through her foot. (National Park Service.)

THE DEATH OF EDOUARD DE LABOULAYE. The 72-year-old spiritual and intellectual "father of the Statue of Liberty" died in Paris of a heart malady in May 1883. Though he did not live to see his magnificent gift to the United States unveiled, he at least lived long enough to see it approach completion. Laboulaye died as a senator of the French Third Republic, and so lived to see at least one of his dreams completed. (National Park Service.)

PRESENTING LADY LIBERTY. On July 4, 1884, the Statue of Liberty was officially presented to the American ambassador, Levi Parsons Morton, in a ceremony in Paris. This scroll, signed by the participants, is a record of the event. Among the signatories is Viscount Ferdinand de Lesseps, who succeeded Laboulaye as president of the Franco-American Union. (National Park Service.)

Three

THE PEDESTAL

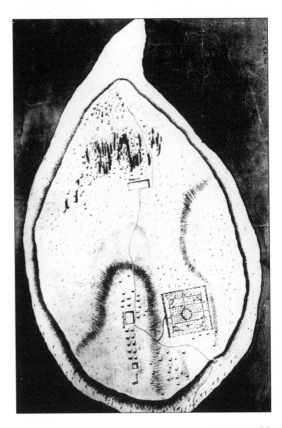

MAP OF BEDLOE'S ISLAND. This survey map of Bedloe's Island was drawn in 1772. The island later became a military post. Auguste Bartholdi thought it was the perfect site for the Statue of Liberty. (National Park Service.)

FORT WOOD, BEDLOE'S ISLAND, 1864. Fort Wood was established in 1811 and was strengthened with rusticated granite stones in 1844. After Gen. William T. Sherman confirmed Fort Wood as the permanent home of the Statue of Liberty in 1877, the garrison moved outside of the fort's walls, and a series of new military buildings was constructed. The island remained in army hands until 1937. (U.S. War Department General Staff.)

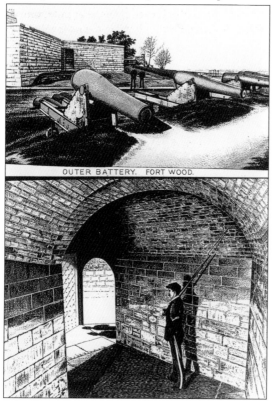

THE FORT WOOD BATTERY AND A GUARD ON DUTY. The top image of this engraving shows the battery of Rodman guns that was set up outside of Fort Wood after the army evacuated the fortress in 1877. The guns remained in place until 1904, when the regular army left the island and was replaced by the Army Signal Corps. The lower sketch shows a soldier on guard duty inside of the walls of Fort Wood. (National Park Service.)

A Bartholdi Design of the Pedestal. In a letter written in 1882, Auguste Bartholdi proposed this pyramidal design for Liberty's pedestal. It reveals how strongly the architecture of ancient Egypt still influenced his views. In another drawing, Bartholdi made the pedestal taller. (National Park Service.)

WILLIAM MAXWELL EVARTS. William M. Evarts (1818–1901) was the leading fund-raiser for the pedestal campaign. As chairman of the American Committee, from 1877 to 1886, he successfully raised more than $323,000. Evarts's presence as chairman brought credibility to the project, and his political and social clout drew support from unlikely quarters and even won an endorsement from Congress in 1877. As a member of the prestigious Union League Club, he drew other wealthy Republican club men into the project, including Theodore Roosevelt Sr., John Jay II, Richard Butler, Sen. Edwin D. Morgan, Chauncey Mitchell Depew, Anson Phelps Stokes, and Richard Morris Hunt. Evarts was a distinguished statesman and lawyer and had served as U.S. attorney general (1868–1869), as U.S. secretary of state (1877–1881), and as a U.S. senator (1885–1891). (National Park Service.)

RICHARD MORRIS HUNT. The Statue of Liberty project seemed to draw talent from every quarter. Not the least of these talented individuals was the New York–based architect Richard Morris Hunt (1828–1895). Hunt, who was preeminent in his field, accepted the commission from the American Committee to design the pedestal. The committee rejected several of his drawings before he won its approval for a final effort in the summer of 1884. Hunt donated his fee to the committee. His other works include the vast Vanderbilt mansion known as Biltmore, the New York Tribune Building, and the Administration Building at the Chicago World's Fair of 1893. (National Park Service.)

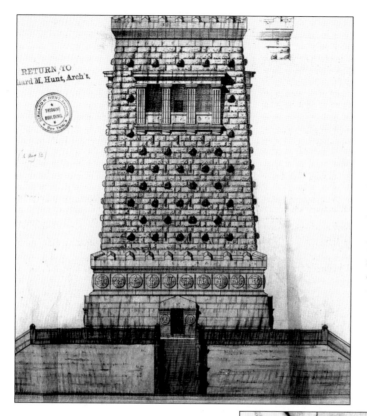

AN EARLY PEDESTAL DRAWING. This drawing of the pedestal from August 1883 distressed the American Committee due to its excessive expense, as Hunt wanted the entire construction to be made of granite. The committee was also displeased with its excessive height. It was duly rejected on these grounds, and Hunt went back to his offices in the New York Tribune Building to produce a scaled-down model for the committee's consideration. (National Park Service.)

THE MODEL OF LIBERTY AND THE PEDESTAL. Richard Morris Hunt diminished the height of the pedestal somewhat and had this model built so that the American Committee could get a better idea of what he was driving at. But the committee was worried by the cost of it (granite being an expensive material) and once again raised objections to its height. (National Park Service.)

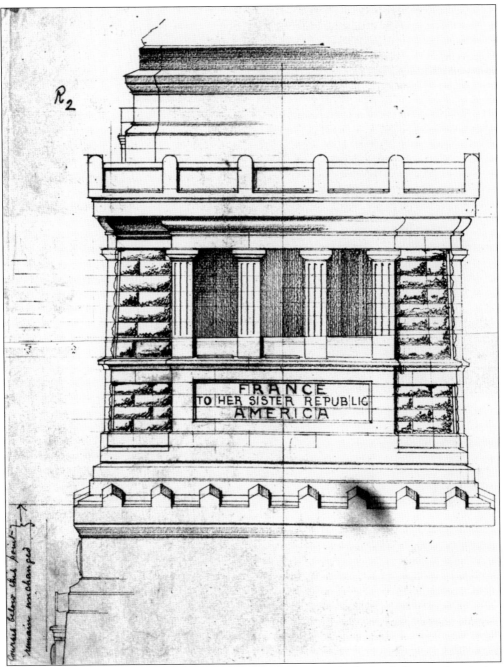

NEARLY DONE. This drawing generally satisfied the committee (only the dedicatory inscription was deleted). The financial savings from such a pedestal were great, since Hunt's new design called for only a façade of granite with far fewer courses than his previous offerings had featured. (National Park Service.)

THE MASONIC CONNECTION: WILLIAM A. BRODIE. The Free and Accepted Masons played an important role in the history of the Statue of Liberty, and this is no less true in the case of the pedestal. Pictured here is William A. Brodie (1841–1917), grand master of the Grand Lodge of New York State. Accompanied by 100 fellow masons, he presided over the pedestal's Masonic consecration at the Laying of the Cornerstone ceremony on August 5, 1884. Among those at his side were deputy master Frank Lawrence and Charles Camp, the lodge's chaplain. (National Park Service.)

REV. CHARLES W. CAMP, GRAND MASONIC CHAPLAIN. In the 1880s, Rev. Dr. Charles William Camp served as the grand chaplain of the New York Lodge of the Masons and also played a role at the Laying of the Cornerstone ceremony with Grand Master Brodie. Years later, Reverend Camp's nephew, Oswald E. Camp, served as superintendent of the Statue of Liberty National Monument (1935–1937) and presided over Liberty's Golden Jubilee on October 28, 1936. (National Park Service.)

The Laying of the Cornerstone. A massive pyramid made of concrete was built inside the walls of old Fort Wood. On this foundation, the granite and concrete pedestal was to be erected. The Freemasons laid the cornerstone on August 5, 1884. On that day, Grand Master Brodie proclaimed, "No institution has done more to promote liberty . . . than freemasonry, and we as a fraternity take an honest pride in depositing the corner-stone of the pedestal of the statue of *Liberty Enlightening the World*." (National Park Service.)

The Masonry Foundation of the Pedestal. Planned and designed by Gen. Charles P. Stone, the concrete foundation was laid inside of Fort Wood from October 1883 to May 1884. The materials used were cement, stones, and sand, all of which were supplied by a New York firm headed by F. Hopkinson Smith, a well-known engineer and novelist. (National Park Service.)

PUCK'S ATTACK ON THE COMMERCIALIZATION OF LIBERTY. This cartoon appeared in *Puck* magazine in 1883. A number of commercial businesses were already selling their products using the Statue of Liberty. (National Park Service.)

A DONATION CERTIFICATE.
Donors to the pedestal campaign were given this handsome certificate in gratitude.
The signatories are American Committee executive directors William M. Evarts (chairman), Richard Butler (secretary), Henry F. Spaulding (treasurer), James W. Drexel, Parke Godwin, V. Mumford Moore, Frederick A. Potts, and James W. Pinchot. (National Park Service.)

LIMELIGHT STARS FOR LIBERTY. Rudolph Aronson of the Casino Theatre arranged this benefit show for the pedestal in 1885. Lillian Russell, Richard Mansfield, and Robert B. Mantell were just a few of the famous actors who performed. (National Park Service.)

BARTHOLDI'S *LION OF BELFORT*. While the Statue of Liberty project was moving along, Auguste Bartholdi produced another colossal piece of sculpture. The *Lion of Belfort* paid tribute to the town of Belfort, which the Prussians failed to vanquish during the Franco-Prussian War. The sandstone lion commemorating the valor of the French defenders was dedicated in 1880. (National Park Service.)

THE TORCH ON DISPLAY IN MADISON SQUARE PARK. The torch was brought to Philadelphia in 1876, where it was unveiled at the U.S. Centennial Exhibition. From 1877 to 1882, it was displayed in New York City's Madison Square Park before being returned to France. (National Park Service.)

The Statue of Liberty Enlightening The World.

Described by the Sculptor BARTHOLDI

Published for the Benefit of the Pedestal Fund
BY THE
NORTH AMERICAN REVIEW
30 LAFAYETTE PLACE,
NEW YORK.

THE PEDESTAL FUND-RAISING BOOK. Raising money for the pedestal became more and more difficult as time pressed on. Distressed by the declining donations for the pedestal, Auguste Bartholdi wrote this short book to aid the American Committee. The text was quickly translated into English and was published by the *North American Review* in 1885. (National Park Service.)

GEN. CHARLES P. STONE. In 1883, when Gen. Charles P. Stone returned to the United States after several years in Egypt, he was immediately hired by the American Committee to construct the foundation and the pedestal. The general worked closely with the committee's executives, architect Richard Morris Hunt, and building contractor David H. King Jr. His assistants were Col. Samuel Lockett and George F. Simpson. At the conclusion of the project, he served as grand marshal of the inaugural parade for the Statue of Liberty on October 28, 1886. A West Point graduate, Charles Pomeroy Stone (1824–1887) had a long military career. He fought in the war with Mexico and in the Civil War; during the latter war, he met with misfortune and eventually resigned his commission. In the 1870s, his ability as a military engineer led to his appointment as chief of public works in the Egyptian army. (National Park Service.)

Four

TO AMERICA

THE ARRIVAL OF THE STATUE OF LIBERTY. This image shows the arrival of the Statue of Liberty in New York Harbor on June 17, 1885. The statue was packed in 214 heavy cases and shipped to the United States on the *Isère*, a warship of the French Navy. The master of the vessel was Lieutenant Commander De Saune, who carried a letter dated May 15, 1885, from Viscount de Lesseps, the president of the Franco-American Union. It instructed him to deliver the cargo to Joseph W. Drexel of the American Committee and to Gen. Charles P. Stone. The ship had set sail from Rouen, France, on May 21, 1885, and in the course of its voyage had met with storms and high winds. By June 2, it had reached Portugal's Azores Islands, where it took on provisions and coal. It departed from the Azores on June 4, and the Atlantic crossing was smooth and pleasant. (National Park Service.)

FRANK LESLIE'S ILLUSTRATED NEWSPAPER

No. 1,553.—Vol. LX.]   NEW YORK—FOR THE WEEK ENDING JUNE 27, 1885.   [PRICE, 10 CENTS.

THE ISÈRE REACHES BEDLOE'S ISLAND. On June 19, 1885, the French frigate *Isère* dropped anchor off Bedloe's Island. On that day, New Yorkers poured into the harbor to welcome the Statue of Liberty to her new home. (National Park Service.)

54

UNLOADING THE ISÈRE. Painted white for service in the tropics, the ship (in the distance on the left) is seen here being unloaded. The ship's officers were given a grand parade from the battery to city hall, where they were fêted at a reception. Furthermore, they were given a sumptuous dinner at Delmonico's restaurant that evening. Throughout their stay, the crew members were treated with warmth and were given many presents. The French Ministry of Marine normally used the Isère and five other frigates to transport troops and munitions to support its colonial activities in Indochina and Madagascar. (National Park Service.)

A CLOSE-UP VIEW OF THE ISÈRE. It took several days to remove the wooden cases bearing the sculptured copper plates, iron posts, armature bars, bolts, and so forth. The cases were transferred from the ship to Bedloe's Island via lighters and handed over to the American consignees. After completing its duty, the Isère set sail for Brest, France, on July 3, 1885. (National Park Service.)

THE FACE OF LIBERTY. This photograph of Liberty was taken in 1886, just after the face had been unpacked from its case. (National Park Service.)

THE PEDESTAL AND DERRICKS.
This drawing shows the extent of the pedestal's construction as of June 6, 1885. Hoisting apparatus called derricks were rigged with tackle and used to lift the construction materials. At several points during the construction, work had to be halted because of the lack of funds. (National Park Service.)

PULITZER TO THE RESCUE.
Despite its undeniable achievements, the American Committee was in an embarrassing position when the Statue of Liberty landed only to find that her pedestal was still unfinished. The sudden intervention of newspaper publisher Joseph Pulitzer in the fund-raising campaign brought welcome relief. Pulitzer offered to print the names of all donors in his newspaper, the *World*. This bold move paid off, for from March to August 1885, he raised the last $100,000 needed, and the pedestal was completed by April 1886. (National Park Service.)

A CONSTRUCTION CREW. Pictured are some of the workmen who built the pedestal and assembled the Statue of Liberty on Bedloe's Island. The photograph was taken at the island in 1886. The large contingent of workmen included many Italian immigrants. (National Park Service.)

ASSEMBLING THE STATUE OF LIBERTY. Beginning in May 1886, Liberty's iron pylon system and its secondary and tertiary extensions were assembled and secured to the anchorage of steel beams embedded in the pedestal's concrete walls and in the foundation below. General Stone designed the anchorage system, and David H. King supervised the workforce. (National Park Service.)

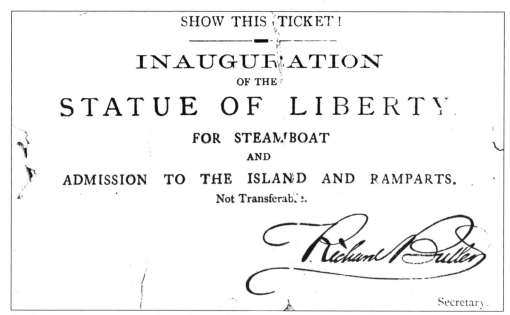

SHOW THIS TICKET!

INAUGURATION
OF THE
STATUE OF LIBERTY.
FOR STEAMBOAT
AND
ADMISSION TO THE ISLAND AND RAMPARTS.
Not Transferable.

Secretary.

AN INVITATION TICKET. This ticket to the Statue of Liberty's inauguration on Bedloe's Island was a treasured item. (National Park Service.)

INAUGURATION

OF THE STATUE OF

LIBERTY ENLIGHTENING THE WORLD.

Order of Exercises

ON BEDLOW'S ISLAND,

Thursday, October 28th, 1886.

THE DEDICATION CEREMONY, OCTOBER 28, 1886. The order of exercises for the dedication of the Statue of Liberty took place in the afternoon and featured music, a prayer, an address by Viscount de Lesseps of the Franco-American Union, a presentation address by William M. Evarts of the American Committee, a salvo from all the guns in the harbor, music, and then the acceptance speech by President Cleveland. Addresses were also made by French consul general W. Albert LeFaivre and Union League Club president Chauncey Mitchell Depew. Auguste Bartholdi and his wife were also in attendance.

UNVEILING OF THE STATUE OF LIBERTY, 1886. Maritime artist Edward Moran, who had learned of the Liberty project in 1876 and met Bartholdi at the Century Club in 1877, did this oil painting. Moran also painted *Commerce of Nations Rendering Homage to Liberty*, *The Statue of Liberty at Night*, and *Reception of the French Steamship Isère in New York Bay*. (National Park Service.)

THE SALUTE TO LIBERTY. This photograph of the salute to Liberty on October 28, 1886, was taken on board the steamer *Patrol*. President Cleveland and some 2,000 dignitaries were on Bedloe's Island when the military and naval salvoes were fired off just before the French flag that covered Liberty's face was removed. (National Park Service.)

PRES. GROVER CLEVELAND. In accepting the Statue of Liberty from the French, President Cleveland declared, "We will not forget that Liberty has here made her home nor shall her chosen altar be neglected. Willing votaries will constantly keep alive its fires and these shall gleam upon the shores of our sister republic . . . until Liberty enlightens the world." (National Park Service.)

A GIFT
FROM
THE PEOPLE OF THE REPUBLIC OF FRANCE
TO THE PEOPLE OF THE UNITED STATES.
THIS STATUE
OF
LIBERTY ENLIGHTENING THE WORLD
COMMEMORATES THE ALLIANCE OF THE TWO NATIONS
IN ACHIEVING THE INDEPENDENCE
OF THE
UNITED STATES OF AMERICA,
AND
ATTESTS THEIR ABIDING FRIENDSHIP.

AUGUSTE BARTHOLDI.
SCULPTOR.

INAUGURATED
OCTOBER 28TH 1886.

THE PRESENTATION TABLET. This tablet of brass is the official presentation tablet of the Statue of Liberty and is on display in the Statue of Liberty exhibit on Liberty Island. (National Park Service.)

FINIS! The sculptor Auguste Bartholdi was hailed by the American people for the triumphant statue of *Liberty Enlightening the World,* and he went home to Paris with a feeling that his dream had at last come true: he had created a colossus grand enough to rival the works of antiquity, a veritable eighth wonder of the world. Most of the praise and adulation went to the sculptor, and the late Edouard de Laboulaye's critical contributions were already fading from popular memory. (National Park Service.)

IMMIGRATION. The Statue of Liberty was admired by a great many visitors to New York as well as by its own residents. But a very special sort of tribute to it came from an unexpected quarter. These were the thousands of poor immigrants entering the United States from the nations of Europe, the Near East, and the Caribbean. They had purchased steamship tickets and traveled in steerage—the cheapest way to sail. The Statue of Liberty was truly an astonishing site to them, classically gowned as she was and gazing with a stern but noble countenance. Many foreigners hadn't the foggiest idea what the colossus represented. Some mistook her for a Christian saint; others fancied that her pedestal might be the tomb of Christopher Columbus. As the years passed, the monument became a legend to immigrants; before leaving the old country, many were told that when they arrived in America, the Statue of Liberty would be there to greet them. (National Park Service.)

Five

THE COLOSSUS
OF NEW YORK

LIBERTY AMONG
THE COLOSSI. At its
completion in 1886, the
Statue of Liberty was
the tallest man-made
structure in the Western
Hemisphere and was
taller than many of
the highest structures
previously erected.
(National Park Service.)

THE WONDER OF NEW YORK. New Yorkers were quite proud of their newest resident. Her sculptor, Bartholdi, had received the "Freedom of the City" award, and a number of places and businesses were at least briefly named for him. (National Park Service.)

MEASURING THE LADY. Liberty's magnificence is demonstrated by her stunning dimensions. She stands 151 feet 1 inch high, and with her 89-foot-high pedestal, she rises 305 feet 1 inch. Her nose is nearly 4 feet long, her right arm is 42 feet long, and the longest ray of her halo is 11 feet 6 inches long. (National Park Service.)

DIMENSIONS
—— OF THE ——
STATUE OF LIBERTY.
·····●●●●●·····

	Ft.	In.
Height from base to torch	151	1
Foundation of pedestal to torch	305	6
Heel to top of hand	111	6
Length of hand	16	5
Index finger	8	0
Circumference at second joint	7	6
Size of finger nail		13x10
Head from chin to cranium	17	3
Head, thickness from ear to ear	10	0
Distance across the eye	2	6
Length of nose	4	6
Right arm, length	42	0
Right arm, greatest thickness	12	0
Thickness of waist	35	0
Width of mouth	3	0
Tablet, length	23	7
" width	13	7
" thickness	2	0

DIMENSIONS OF PEDESTAL.

	Ft.	In.
Height of pedestal	89	0
Square sides at base, each	62	0
" " " top, "	40	0
Grecian columns, above base	72	8

DIMENSIONS OF FOUNDATION.

	Ft.	In.
Height of foundation	65	0
Square sides at bottom	91	0
" " " top	66	7

The statue weighs 450,000 pounds or 225 tons. The bronze alone weighs 200,000 pounds. Forty persons can stand comfortably in the head, and the torch will hold twelve people.

The number of steps in the statue, from the pedestal to the head, is 154, and the ladder leading up through the extended right arm to the torch has 54 rounds.

FROM THE CROW'S-NEST. The panoramic vistas from the Statue of Liberty's quivering torch delighted thousands of visitors in the 30 years following her unveiling. But this treat came to a halt permanently in July of 1916, following the Black Tom wharf explosions in nearby Jersey City. Though Liberty's right arm suffered only minor damage from the explosions, her caretakers reached the conclusion that it was safer to keep it closed. (National Park Service.)

Statue of Liberty Excursions

Bedlow's Island, N.Y. Harbor

Bartholdi Statue of Liberty.

STEAMER "FALCON"

Leaves Barge Office, Battery Pier.
Terminus of all the Elevated Roads,
Broadway Cars, Etc.

9, 10, 11, 12 A. M., 1, 2, 3, 4, 5   P. M.

EVERY DAY.

Extra and Later Trips on Sundays & Holidays.

NO ADMISSION CHARGED TO STATUE.

THE FERRY TO BEDLOE'S ISLAND. The *Falcon* was one of the very first steamers to ferry sightseers to the great statue on Bedloe's Island. Thousands of visitors, especially out-of-towners, made the trip. (National Park Service.)

STATUE OF LIBERTY BY NIGHT, NEW YORK CITY.

THE LIBERTY LIGHTHOUSE IN 1902. In its early years, the Statue of Liberty served as a lighthouse as well as a monument. The U.S. Lighthouse Board operated an electrical lighting plant on Bedloe's Island and had installed nine lamps inside the torch and a few more to illuminate the statue's body from below. The effect was not really helpful to sea captains from afar, and Liberty's 15 years as a harbor beacon were ended by March 1902.

LIBERTY'S LIFT. The Otis Elevator Company installed the Statue of Liberty's first elevator in 1907. Located in the pedestal, it was operated by cable pulleys and allowed visitors the luxury of a pleasant ride up to the top of the pedestal before they had to face the narrow steps of the circular staircase inside the statue. (National Park Service.)

CABLES AND CARETAKERS. The elevator had to be operated by a caretaker. The caretaker was also responsible for keeping the monument swept out and for making sure that the light of a paraffin lamp brightened the visitors' trip to the top. (National Park Service.)

NIGHT WATCH. Liberty has been faithfully on watch in the harbor of New York since 1886 and has seen millions of people and thousands of vessels and aircraft pass by. (National Park Service.)

THE SOLDIERS OF FORT WOOD. For more than 50 years following Liberty's dedication, soldiers were stationed at Fort Wood on Bedloe's Island. This 1884 tintype image brings before our eyes a day when two soldiers and a lad posed for a cameraman on one of the Rodman cannons that stood outside the fortress's walls. The pedestal was still under construction. (National Park Service.)

THE CARETAKER AND HIS FAMILY.
The American Committee hired James McLaughlin to be the caretaker and watchman for the statue and pedestal at night. In this 1884 tintype, McLaughlin poses in front of one of the fort's great guns with his wife, Elizabeth, and their children. (National Park Service.)

JAMES MCLAUGHLIN AND FOUR GENTLEMEN. Liberty's caretaker, James McLaughlin (standing on the right), is pictured with four gentlemen who visited the island c. 1884. (National Park Service.)

CASTLE GARDEN AND THE STATUE OF LIBERTY. This *c.* 1888 image shows Liberty far in the distance and the famous Castle Garden Immigrant Depot in the foreground. Eight million immigrants passed through Castle Garden during its 35 years of operation. Closed in 1890, the New York State immigrant landing depot was soon replaced by the federally operated Ellis Island Immigrant Station. Castle Garden is now called Castle Clinton. (National Park Service.)

BEDLOE'S ISLAND AND ELLIS ISLAND. This photograph was taken on Bedloe's Island *c.* 1895. The Ellis Island Immigrant Station can be seen across the water. Liberty's caretaker, James McLaughlin, poses in front of some Rodman cannons with two soldiers. (National Park Service.)

IMMIGRANTS TO AMERICA. Ships laden with immigrants had to stop for an inspection by New York State quarantine inspectors before being allowed to sail past the Statue of Liberty on the way to their piers of Manhattan and Hoboken. (National Park Service.)

EMMA LAZARUS. Poet Emma Lazarus (1849–1887) wrote the celebrated sonnet "The New Colossus," which hails Liberty as the "mother of exiles." Lazarus's poem became well known to the public in the 1930s thanks to writer Louis Adamic, the media, and the National Park Service. (National Park Service.)

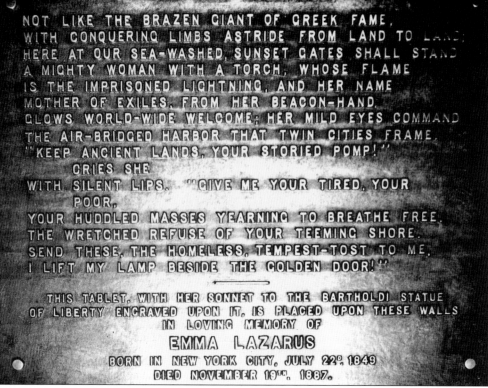

THE NEW COLOSSUS.

NOT LIKE THE BRAZEN GIANT OF GREEK FAME,
WITH CONQUERING LIMBS ASTRIDE FROM LAND TO LAND;
HERE AT OUR SEA-WASHED, SUNSET GATES SHALL STAND
A MIGHTY WOMAN WITH A TORCH, WHOSE FLAME
IS THE IMPRISONED LIGHTNING, AND HER NAME
MOTHER OF EXILES. FROM HER BEACON-HAND,
GLOWS WORLD-WIDE WELCOME; HER MILD EYES COMMAND
THE AIR-BRIDGED HARBOR THAT TWIN CITIES FRAME.
"KEEP ANCIENT LANDS, YOUR STORIED POMP!"
    CRIES SHE
WITH SILENT LIPS. "GIVE ME YOUR TIRED, YOUR
    POOR,
YOUR HUDDLED MASSES YEARNING TO BREATHE FREE,
THE WRETCHED REFUSE OF YOUR TEEMING SHORE.
SEND THESE, THE HOMELESS, TEMPEST-TOST TO ME,
I LIFT MY LAMP BESIDE THE GOLDEN DOOR!"

THIS TABLET, WITH HER SONNET TO THE BARTHOLDI STATUE
OF LIBERTY ENGRAVED UPON IT, IS PLACED UPON THESE WALLS
IN LOVING MEMORY OF
EMMA LAZARUS
BORN IN NEW YORK CITY, JULY 22°, 1849
DIED NOVEMBER 19TH, 1887.

"THE NEW COLOSSUS." Emma Lazarus wrote this poem in aid of the pedestal fund in 1883. It was first read publicly at the National Academy of Design in December 1883. The words were inscribed on this bronze tablet in 1903, and the tablet was put on display at the monument. (National Park Service.)

BARTHOLDI IN HIS LATER YEARS. Famed sculptor Auguste Bartholdi remained busy in his later years. He is seen here c. 1895 working on a bust of politician Claudius Guichard in his Paris studio. (National Park Service.)

THE DEATH OF THE SCULPTOR.
Frederic-Auguste Bartholdi died in
Paris on October 4, 1904, at the
age of 70. He had been afflicted
with tuberculosis for three years.
He was buried in Montparnasse
Cemetery. Pictured here is the
statue of Bartholdi made in 1907
by the artist Hubert Louis-Noel.
It stands in Colmar.

THE AMERICANIZATION CAMPAIGN.
The Statue of Liberty, long a potent
symbol to immigrants, has often been used
to encourage them to become U.S. citizens.
(National Park Service.)

LIBERTY STATUE STANDS TEST.

Only a Few Bolts Ripped Off—Loss on Island, $100,000.

After the United States Army engineers had surveyed the Statue of Liberty and the buildings on Bedlow's Island yesterday Captain A. T. Clifton, the commandant of the Signal Corps which is stationed there, said the repairs there would cost about $100,000.

It would take about ten days to make the temporary repairs, such as fitting the casings of the windows in the houses and the doors which had been blown off by the explosion, he said, and during that period the public would be excluded from the island.

Captain Clifton went on to say that the buildings were not damaged, with the exception of the western storehouse, a corrugated iron structure, which had been ripped to pieces by the concussion. The main structure of the Statue of Liberty practically escaped uninjured, as well as the power plant which provides the light. About 100 iron bolts in the inner shell of the statue had been ripped off and the base and outer envelope of the statue had been chipped a little with the shrapnel from the barges at Black Tom Island.

Captain Clifton stated that the officers' houses now had no windows, frames or doors, and were being blocked up with tarred paper until the proper materials could be obtained. Several of the shells

SABOTAGE AT BLACK TOM. The Black Tom wharf explosions at the Jersey docks on July 30, 1916, killed seven people and set off dangerous fires that were only gradually brought under control. Liberty's right arm suffered minor damage. This was the first major act of terrorism to be perpetrated near the Statue of Liberty. The saboteurs were German agents. This article was published in *The New York Times* on August 1, 1916. (National Park Service.)

THE GODDESS AND THE BOY SCOUT. This World War I fund-raising poster for the Liberty Loan strongly identified the goddess of Liberty with American principles. (National Park Service.)

FOOD RATIONING IN WORLD WAR I. Although food rationing was not greatly pressed during World War I, the Food Administration made an effort to persuade Americans to waste nothing. Here, immigrants are called on to play their part. (National Park Service.)

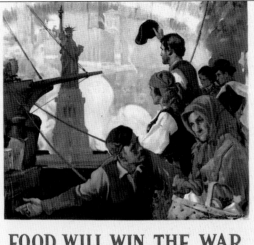

THE WORLD'S LARGEST WREATH. Quite appropriately, the world's largest wreath (according to its creators) was laid at the world's largest statue. This occurred on Memorial Day, May 30, 1921, to honor America's war veterans. The wreath weighed 1,500 pounds and had a circumference of 97 feet. (National Park Service.)

A NATIONAL MONUMENT.
President Calvin Coolidge (pictured here in 1927) declared the Statue of Liberty a national monument under the care of the War Department on October 15, 1924. National monuments are created under the provisions of the Antiquities Act of 1906. (National Park Service.)

AUTOGIROS OVER BEDLOE'S ISLAND. Aviators have found Lady Liberty appealing, as shown in this photograph taken *c.* 1929. (National Archives.)

THE CIRCULAR STAIRCASE. Here is a 1930s view of the circular staircase that took visitors up to the crown of the Statue of Liberty. (National Park Service.)

OPENING DAY AT THE STATUE OF LIBERTY SOUVENIR STAND. Pictured here are Aaron Hill (wearing the hat) with his wife, Evelyn, and their children James and Constance Hill. On the far left is Evelyn Hill's cousin. The photograph was taken in 1931. James Hill and his son, Bradford, still operate the island's concession, which now includes a restaurant and gift shop. (Courtesy of the Hill Family.)

FORT WOOD FROM THE AIR. The military post at Fort Wood can be seen in this *c.* 1932 aerial photograph of Bedloe's Island. (National Park Service.)

FORT WOOD'S ENTRANCE. This 1934 photograph shows Supt. George Palmer inspecting the main sally port entrance to Fort Wood and the mechanism that opened its heavy doors. The National Park Service took over the statue in 1933. (National Park Service.)

80

ON THE OBSERVATION BALCONY.
Foreign visitors accompany Supt. George
Palmer at the top of the pedestal in 1935.
(National Park Service.)

INSIDE THE LADY'S ARM. This ranger stands near the highest rung of the ladder leading to the torch of the Statue of Liberty. The year is 1935. (National Park Service.)

A CLOSE AERIAL VIEW OF THE ISLAND. This photograph of Bedloe's Island, Liberty, and Fort Wood was taken in the late 1920s. (National Park Service.)

NEW YORK HARBOR FROM A GREAT WAY OFF. This is how the harbor appeared on October 7, 1932. In the foreground, from left to right, are Black Tom wharf, Ellis Island, and Bedloe's Island. Beyond those, from left to right, are Manhattan, Brooklyn, and Governors Island. (National Park Service.)

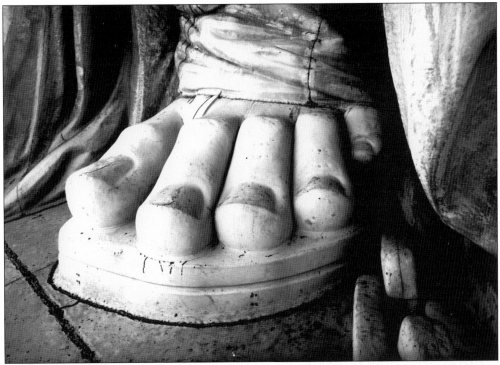

THE RIGHT FOOT OF FREEDOM. Liberty's colossal feet are shod in Roman sandals. (National Park Service.)

THE BROKEN SHACKLE AND CHAIN. Difficult to see except from above, this symbol of liberty represents the end of servitude, tyranny, and oppression. This photograph was taken in 1937. (National Park Service.)

A Portion of the Torch. Here, the light of Liberty is seen from one of its several angles. (National Park Service.)

Liberty's Drapery. The gowns Liberty wears are actually a *stola* and *palla*. These toga-like garments of ancient Rome were worn by noblewomen; they also draped the figures of that civilization's goddesses. (National Park Service.)

THE FINGER, HALO, AND TABLET.
The statue's halo of seven spikes is
called a *nimbus* in classical art and
adorns the heads of deities and saints.
The tablet is inscribed with the date
of the Declaration of Independence.
(National Park Service.)

OSWALD CAMP. Oswald E. Camp
was the superintendent of the Statue
of Liberty National Monument from
1935 to 1937. He enjoyed a long
career in the National Park Service.
(National Park Service.)

THE HARBOR, MARCH 11, 1940. This aerial view of New York Harbor shows Bedloe's Island in the foreground, Ellis Island just above it to the left, and a sweeping view of lower Manhattan, including its Hudson River piers at the upper left. (National Park Service.)

THE EAST PIER AND FERRIES. This 1938 photograph shows the East Pier of Bedloe's Island and the Sutton Line's ferries, the *Islander* and the *Madisonville*. The ferries served thousands of tourists who visited the Statue of Liberty. (National Park Service.)

Six

THE GOLDEN JUBILEE

MISS LIBERTY'S GOLDEN JUBILEE.
On October 28, 1936, the goddess of
Liberty celebrated her 50th anniversary.
The celebration attracted thousands.
Events on the island included a liberty
essay contest under the sponsorship of
the Ladies Auxiliary of the Veterans of
Foreign Wars. (National Park Service.)

DRESSED FOR HER JUBILEE.
Liberty and her comrade Old Glory stand high above an array of patriotic flags. (National Park Service.)

THE INDIANAPOLIS. The U.S. naval cruiser *Indianapolis* was anchored off of Bedloe's Island and played a key role in the tributes to the Statue of Liberty on her Golden Jubilee. (Department of the Navy.)

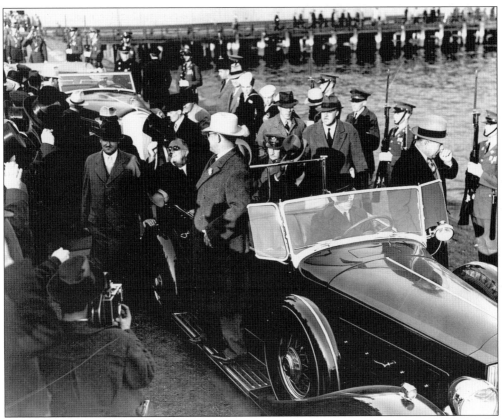

A MOTORCAR PARADE ON BEDLOE'S ISLAND. Pres. Franklin D. Roosevelt presided over the Golden Jubilee. (National Park Service.)

SOLDIERS BEARING FLAGS. With the USS *Indianapolis* anchored nearby, the military celebrated Liberty's 50th anniversary. (National Park Service.)

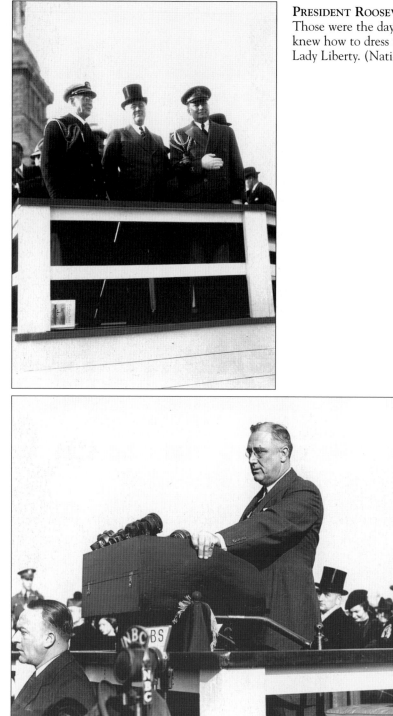

PRESIDENT ROOSEVELT IN A TOP HAT. Those were the days when a president knew how to dress in the presence of Lady Liberty. (National Park Service.)

PRESIDENT ROOSEVELT'S ADDRESS. At Liberty's 1936 Golden Jubilee, the president declared that the covenant to preserve Liberty and "her chosen altar" had not been broken in the 50 years that the statue had made her home in America. (National Park Service.)

NBC's Jubilee Broadcast.
NBC made this radio broadcast from
the torch on October 28, 1936. From
left to right stand Joseph S. Bell,
Antonia Dmitrieff, and newsman
John B. Kennedy. Kennedy also
interviewed Superintendent Camp
from the torch. (National Park
Service.)

Harold Ickes. Secretary of the Interior Harold Ickes, as head of the National Park Service,
also made a few remarks on Liberty's golden day. On the far right (waving his hat) is Fiorello
LaGuardia, the mayor of New York City. (National Park Service.)

A Man and the Colossus. Park guide William Webb agreed to be photographed in a few tricky positions at the feet of the colossus *c.* 1936. (National Park Service.)

Liberty Cartoons of 1937. Superintendent Camp gathered these cartoons during his last year of working at Bedloe's Island. (National Park Service.)

THE 51ST ANNIVERSARY.
Liberty's Golden Jubilee was such a success that the National Park Service decided to celebrate the statue's 51st anniversary as well. The celebration included a tribute to the U.S. Constitution on its 150th anniversary. An altar of Liberty was also constructed in honor of the statue. Qualified foreigners received their citizenship in a special ceremony. (National Park Service.)

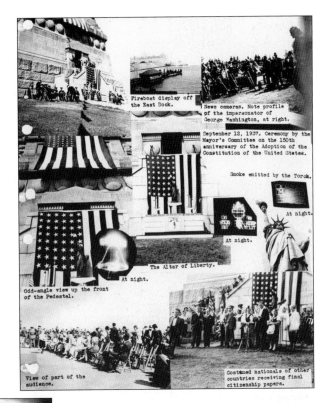

THE PARIS UNIVERSAL EXPOSITION OF 1937.
The French State Railways advertisement featured Liberty and the Eiffel Tower to attract Americans to visit the great Paris Expo of 1937. The exposition featured pavilions from many countries, including England, Canada, Germany, Italy, and the United States, and was attended by 34 million visitors. (National Park Service.)

93

BETTY GRABLE AND CHIQUITA. Pictured are film star Betty Grable (right) and her friend Chiquita on the observation balcony in 1936. (National Park Service.)

REMOVING THE SPIKES. These three workmen are securing tackle to a derrick on Liberty's head. This was done to remove the enormous spikes that form Liberty's halo. The photograph was taken in 1938. (National Park Service.)

THE SPIKES REMOVED. Liberty's *nimbus* (halo) spikes were taken down for cleaning and repair work during the 1938 restoration, which was done to prepare the statue for the New York World's Fair of 1939. (National Park Service.)

THE STAIRS IN THE PEDESTAL. This was part of the staircase system that visitors used to climb upward into the pedestal to reach the circular stairs inside the statue. (National Park Service.)

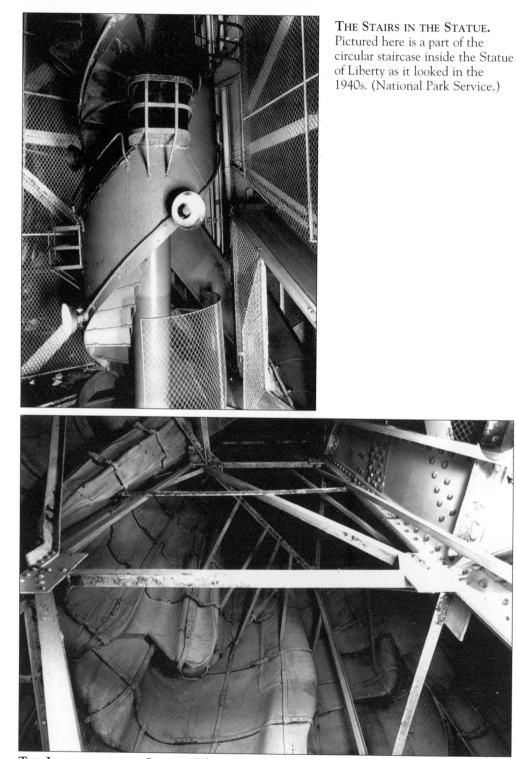

THE STAIRS IN THE STATUE. Pictured here is a part of the circular staircase inside the Statue of Liberty as it looked in the 1940s. (National Park Service.)

THE INTERIOR OF THE STATUE. Liberty's magnificent framework system, armature bars, and copper plates are seen in this 1940s image. (National Park Service.)

Seven

AMERICA'S GREAT LADY

THE 55TH ANNIVERSARY. On October 28, 1941, the Ladies Auxiliary of the Veterans of Foreign Wars celebrated Liberty's 55th anniversary with ceremonies on Bedloe's Island. Pictured here, from left to right, are the following: Count Jacques de Saye; soloist Lucy Monroe; the auxiliary's national president, Alice M. Donahue; and the Veterans of Foreign Wars' commander in chief, Max Singer. (National Park Service.)

VISITORS AT FORT WOOD. In 1943, a ranger shows visitors the old iron chain and gateway entrance to Fort Wood. The old army prison was located here. (National Park Service.)

TOURISTS LOOKING DOWN FROM THE CROWN. This photograph was taken in 1943. (National Park Service.)

ALLIED SAILORS VISIT THE STATUE.
With World War II on, a good
many allied warships called at the
port of New York, and thousands
of foreign sailors were given shore
leave to enjoy the metropolis. One
of their favorite attractions was the
Statue of Liberty. Here, two sailors,
one English and one Russian, pose
in front of the pedestal in 1943.
(Department of the Navy.)

LIBERTY WORKS FOR VICTORY.
During World War II, Liberty played
an important role in the selling of War
Bonds. (National Park Service.)

A GI IN COLMAR, FRANCE. Pictured here is Cpl. Fred Boone with Auguste Bartholdi's original models of the statues of *Liberty Enlightening the World* and *Egypt Carrying the Light to Asia*. This photograph was taken on February 17, 1945, following the liberation of France. (U.S. Army Signal Corps, James W. Todd, Colmar, France, 1945.)

LIBERTY'S LIGHT SWITCH. In this photograph, taken April 9, 1945, Supt. George A. Palmer shows the master electric switch of the Statue of Liberty's lighting system. The Westinghouse Electric Company installed a brighter lighting system at the monument that spring. The lights of the statue were kept off during the wartime blackout. (National Park Service.)

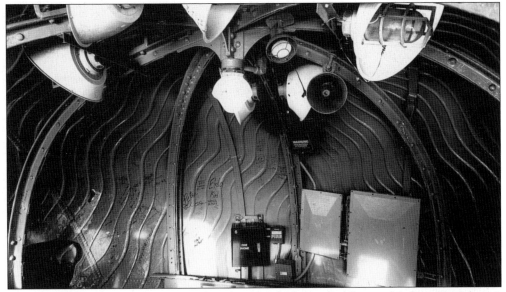

ELECTRIC LAMPS IN THE CROWN. This photograph shows the electrical lighting in Liberty's crown in the 1940s. (National Park Service.)

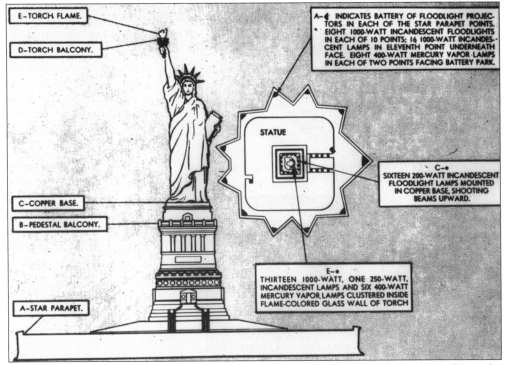

E–TORCH FLAME.

D–TORCH BALCONY.

A–◀ INDICATES BATTERY OF FLOODLIGHT PROJECTORS IN EACH OF THE STAR PARAPET POINTS. EIGHT 1000-WATT INCANDESCENT FLOODLIGHTS IN EACH OF 10 POINTS; 16 1000-WATT INCANDESCENT LAMPS IN ELEVENTH POINT UNDERNEATH FACE. EIGHT 400-WATT MERCURY VAPOR LAMPS IN EACH OF TWO POINTS FACING BATTERY PARK.

STATUE

C–●
SIXTEEN 200-WATT INCANDESCENT FLOODLIGHT LAMPS MOUNTED IN COPPER BASE, SHOOTING BEAMS UPWARD.

C–COPPER BASE.

B–PEDESTAL BALCONY.

E–●
THIRTEEN 1000-WATT, ONE 250-WATT, INCANDESCENT LAMPS AND SIX 400-WATT MERCURY VAPOR LAMPS CLUSTERED INSIDE FLAME-COLORED GLASS WALL OF TORCH

A–STAR PARAPET.

LIBERTY'S NEW LIGHTING SYSTEM. This drawing, released on April 9, 1945, shows the arrangement of the exterior lighting system, which was modernized by the addition of 96 incandescent floodlights. A combination of mercury vapor lamps and incandescent bulbs brightened the torch. Miss Liberty's floodlights, which had been extinguished since Pearl Harbor, were relighted as a victory signal when Germany and Japan surrendered. (National Park Service.)

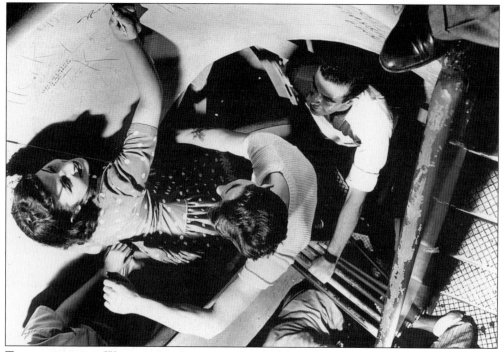

TOURISTS ON THE WAY TO THE CROWN. During the 1946 season, tourists pause to leave their marks on the monument. (National Park Service.)

A POSTWAR PATRIOTIC GATHERING. The French vice consul general presided over this exciting event on February 15, 1947. (National Park Service.)

TOURISTS LINE UP FOR LIBERTY.
This 1947 photograph shows the
long line to enter the Statue of
Liberty. (National Park Service.)

VISITORS PAUSE FOR REFRESHMENTS AND VIEWS. This photograph was taken in 1947.

AN AERIAL VIEW, C. 1950. Portions of New York Harbor, Bedloe's Island, Ellis Island, Jersey City, and Manhattan are seen here. (National Park Service.)

TOURISTS ON THE BALCONY. Tourists crowd on the observation balcony at the top of the pedestal in this photograph from the 1950s. (Jack E. Boucher, National Park Service.)

AN ELEVATOR QUEUE. This photograph shows the elevator service in the pedestal in the 1950s. (National Park Service.)

THE "HANDS ACROSS THE SEA" BROADCAST. On January 27, 1950, this radio broadcast from New York to Paris was made direct from the Statue of Liberty over the RKO local radio station, WOR. Announcer John Wingate hosted a program that featured two Hollywood film stars, a French chanteuse, and the Broadway star of *Miss Liberty*. The celebrities seen in this photograph are, from left to right, actors Franchot Tone and Burgess Meredith (in the foreground) and singer Edith Piaf and stage actress Allyn McLerie (in the background). The uniformed official at the rear left is Simeon H. Pickering, a historical aide at the Statue of Liberty. (National Park Service.)

LOOKING UPWARD. Standing on the observation balcony of the pedestal, a park ranger and a group of tourists take a glance at the Statue of Liberty looming above them. (National Park Service.)

BEDLOE'S ISLAND. This 1950s aerial view of Bedloe's Island shows the monument, the star-shaped Fort Wood, the mall, the dock, buildings occupied by the park service, the restaurant and gift concession, and the old army houses. (National Park Service.)

LIBERTY AND THE NEW JERSEY SHORE. The Statue of Liberty and her island are located off the shore of New Jersey. (National Park Service.)

THE 714,346TH VISITOR. On October 12, 1954, Statue of Liberty Supt. Newell Foster presented a statuette of Liberty to the park's 714,346th visitor, Mrs. R. E. Hendrix of Columbia, North Carolina. (National Park Service.)

A HARBOR VIEW. Theodore Donaldson took this photograph of the Statue of Liberty and New York Harbor. (National Park Service.)

HAPPY 70TH ANNIVERSARY. On October 28, 1956, the Statue of Liberty received this cake to celebrate the 70th anniversary of her unveiling. (National Park Service.)

FROM BEDLOE'S TO "LIBERTY ISLAND." On October 28, 1956, the name of Bedloe's Island was changed to Liberty Island. Here, Secretary of the Interior Fred A. Seaton stands next to seven-year-old Eileen Dreieler as she unveils a facsimile of the plaque announcing the official name change. In spite of the change, many locals still call it Bedloe's Island. (National Park Service.)

A HIGH SCHOOL VISIT IN 1956. This high school group from North Carolina made a donation to build the American Museum of Immigration, which was to be constructed inside the walls of Fort Wood. The students at the lower level are holding the Liberty Island plaque. (National Park Service.)

A REAR VIEW. This photograph provides a fairly close view of Liberty's elegant Roman drapery. (National Park Service.)

the **A**merican **M**useum of **I**mmigration

STATUE OF LIBERTY, U.S.A.

THE AMERICAN MUSEUM OF IMMIGRATION. The fund-raising campaign to build this museum at the base of the pedestal began in 1955 and received support from President Eisenhower and Vice President Nixon as well as from entertainers such as Edward G. Robinson and Ed Sullivan. The group also sponsored the name change of Bedloe's Island to Liberty Island. The museum was planned by experts, including Alden Stevens and Thomas Pitkin of the National Park Service, and by private fund-raisers led by Alexander Hamilton, Gen. Ulysses Grant III, and Pierre S. DuPont III. (National Park Service.)

ARMY HOUSES. This photograph shows one of the old army houses as it looked just prior to being demolished. Fittingly, the photograph was taken on Armistice Day, November 11, 1956. (National Park Service.)

MANHATTAN, BROOKLYN, AND GOVERNORS ISLAND. This aerial photograph of the harbor, taken on December 8, 1961, also shows the Hudson River at the upper left and the Brooklyn Bridge spanning the East River at the upper right. (Port of New York Authority.)

THE SS *UNITED STATES* AND THE STATUE OF LIBERTY. This photograph shows the SS *United States* passing the Statue of Liberty at noon on August 22, 1958. (Port of New York Authority.)

THE RMS *QUEEN MARY* PASSES BY. Great Britain's magnificent steamship, the RMS *Queen Mary*, passes Miss Liberty on November 26, 1964.

THE MUSEUM EXCAVATION. These photographs were taken *c.* 1961. They show the excavating work that was done in preparation for the construction of the American Museum of Immigration (AMI). The plans for the museum called for its construction at the base of the pedestal.(National Park Service.)

A VIEW OF THE PEDESTAL AND PROMENADES. This is a view of the pedestal, its observation balcony, and the three outer promenade levels atop Fort Wood as they appear today. (National Park Service.)

A DOWNWARD VIEW FROM ABOVE THE CROWN. Liberty and the 11-pointed, star-shaped Fort Wood make an impressive image in this 1981 aerial photograph. (National Park Service.)

THE DEDICATION OF THE AMERICAN MUSEUM OF IMMIGRATION. Pres. Richard M. Nixon, First Lady Pat Nixon, and Secretary of the Interior Rogers C. B. Morton are shown at the festivities on Liberty Island on September 26, 1972. On that day, the president dedicated the American Museum of Immigration. (National Park Service.)

INSIDE THE AMERICAN MUSEUM OF IMMIGRATION. These displays highlight the contributions to the United States made by immigrants who have come from France, Scotland, and Hungary. Famous immigrants featured here are E. I. DuPont, Andrew Carnegie, Alexander Graham Bell, and Joseph Pulitzer. (National Park Service.)

115

THE TABLET. The inscription on Liberty's tablet can easily be read in this photograph. It reads July 4, 1776, in commemoration of the Declaration of Independence. The tablet signifies America's freedom from England as well as its constitutional democracy and the rule of law. (National Park Service.)

A CIRCLE OF FREEDOM. Photographer Francisco Hidalgo took this exceptional photograph from the top of the torch. (National Park Service.)

Eight

FORTRESS
OF FREEDOM

PRESIDENT REAGAN LAUNCHES THE RESTORATION CAMPAIGN FOR LIBERTY. In May 1982, Pres. Ronald Reagan chose industrialist Lee A. Iacocca to lead the fund-raising campaign to restore the aging Statue of Liberty; Ellis Island was also included in the campaign. A 1981 study carried out by French engineers showed that the statue was in poor condition. The president's choice of Iacocca was a brilliant one, for the chairman of Chrysler eventually raised more than $500 million. (National Park Service. Photograph by James Oesch.)

THE LADY NEEDS CLEANING.
This photograph gives an idea of the state Liberty was in when President Reagan and Lee Iacocca began the effort to restore the monument to its former glory. (National Park Service.)

THE SUPPLY RAMP. The restoration of such a huge piece of outdoor sculpture as the Statue of Liberty required uncommon arrangements. This image shows the 400-foot-long supply ramp that went from the water's edge to the base of the pedestal. (National Park Service.)

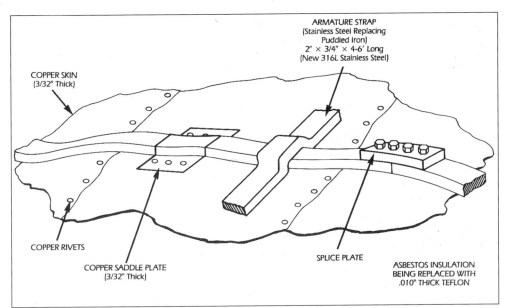

Labels on the diagram:

ARMATURE STRAP
(Stainless Steel Replacing
Puddled Iron)
2″ × 3/4″ × 4-6′ Long
(New 316L Stainless Steel)

COPPER SKIN
(3/32″ Thick)

COPPER RIVETS

COPPER SADDLE PLATE
(3/32″ Thick)

SPLICE PLATE

ASBESTOS INSULATION
BEING REPLACED WITH
.010″ THICK TEFLON

RESTORING LIBERTY'S MIGHTY ARMATURE. This drawing shows the statue's armature system and highlights the replacement of almost all of the 1,800 original iron straps with stainless steel and the replacement of the asbestos insulation between the copper plates and the straps with Teflon. (National Park Service.)

RESTORATION DETAILS. This view from the torch shows the part of the scaffold that surrounded the statue. The restoration process including pressure washing the entire statue and mending the cracks, tears, and blemishes of her sculptured copper form; replacing the iron armature bars with bars of steel; and removing the spikes above her crown for a thorough cleaning.

AT CLOSE QUARTERS. The aluminum scaffold allowed restorers to clean the statue's skin and make all necessary repairs. (National Park Service.)

THE OLD TORCH AND FLAME. Pictured here is the old torch before it was taken down. The famous light of Liberty had to be permanently removed due to its irreparable condition. Deigned by Eugène Viollet-le-Duc and Auguste Bartholdi, it was the oldest part of the Statue of Liberty. It was removed on July 4, 1984, and replaced by a new flame made in exactly the same way. (National Park Service.)

THE NEW TORCH AND FLAME.
The new torch is an exact replica of the old one and is based entirely on the work of Viollet-le-Duc and Bartholdi. The only difference is that this torch's copper flame is covered in gold. Both the old and new torches are 16 feet high and weigh 3,600 pounds. Frank DePalo, a member of the park's Museum Services Division, took this photograph. (National Park Service.)

THE WORLD'S TALLEST SCAFFOLD.
From 1983 to 1986, Liberty was encompassed by the world's tallest freestanding scaffold ever built; it was 300 feet high. The scaffold was designed by Universal Builders Supply, a company located in Mount Vernon, New York. This photograph was taken in January 1986, just after the new torch was put in Liberty's hand. Several weeks after this photograph was taken, the scaffold was removed. (National Park Service.)

LIBERTY RESTORED. This photograph was taken in April 1986. Liberty bears aloft her new torch and flame, and the wonderful scaffold is no more. (National Park Service.)

THE GODDESS OF DEMOCRACY. Inspired by America's goddess of Liberty, anti-communist Chinese revolutionaries built a goddess of Democracy in Beijing's Tiananmen Square in May 1989. The 28-foot-high statue was made of Styrofoam, wires, and plaster. It was destroyed by a Chinese Army tank during the Tiananmen massacre. (National Park Service.)

THE KEEPER OF THE FLAME.
Vincent DiPietro, the park's education specialist, took this amazing photograph of Charlie DeLeo perched atop Liberty's flame. DeLeo was known as the "Keeper of the Flame" because he was the maintenance man assigned to care for the flame, the torch, and the whole statue from 1972 to 1999. This photograph was taken in December 1994. (Vincent DiPietro, National Park Service.)

LIBERTY AND THE TWIN TOWERS. This photograph of the Statue of Liberty and the World Trade Center was taken in 1982. When Liberty was built, she was the tallest structure in New York City and the Western Hemisphere. But as the years passed, skyscrapers were constructed in Manhattan that overreached the magnificent statue's height. The World Trade Center, completed in 1973, was the tallest of the lot. (National Park Service.)

THE TERRORIST ATTACKS OF TUESDAY, SEPTEMBER 11, 2001. The devastating airplane attacks on the World Trade Center took place as most of the employees of the Statue of Liberty and Ellis Island were going to work. Many employees, including the author of this book, were caught in the battleground of Lower Manhattan that smoky Tuesday morning. The Statue of Liberty and Ellis Island were immediately closed, and those employees who had made it to work that morning were sent home.

Expand Sprinkler Systems

Install Emergency
Fire Standpipe System

Upgrade Building
Management & Alarm
Control Systems

Expand Smoke Detection &
Speaker Strobe Systems

Install Viewing Gallery
in Ceiling at 6P Level

Install Additional Exit Signs &
Emergency Lighting

Enhance Lighting Levels

Install Accessible
Ramp at 2P Level

(2) New Exit Doors at East
& West Face of Pedestal
Leading to Sally Port Exit

(2) New Temporary
Wood Egress Stairs

CURTAILED PUBLIC ACCESS TO THE STATUE OF LIBERTY. The Statue of Liberty National Monument was completely closed beginning on September 11, 2001. On December 19, 2001, Ellis Island was reopened, and on August 3, 2004, the Statue of Liberty's pedestal and its museum were reopened to the public following a fund-raising campaign led by the Statue of Liberty–Ellis Island Foundation. (National Park Service.)

The Statue of Liberty Collectors Club

Vol. 13,

Spring/Summer 2004

"Give me your tired, your poor
your huddled masses yearning to breathe fre
The wretched refuse of your teeming s
Send these homeless, tempest-tost to n
I lift my lamp beside the golden

Introducing Liberty Classifieds

Start increasing your collection or selling your duplicates.

This is not eBay, but a real place where buyer and seller are put together with no fees. No auction, just classifieds of Statue of Liberty antiques and collectibles.

Go to: http://classifieds.statueofliberty.info/ and register. It's fast and free.
- No fee to buy or sell.
- Your e-mail address is never visible on the web site, meaning NO SPAM!
- Classifieds are visible for up to 60 days, re-submitting is free!

You can:
* Find new items!
* List item with 1 picture!
* Contact & negotiate with the seller directly!
* Look at ads that are most recently listed!
* Look at most popular ads!
* Payment can be made in any form the seller accepts!

Next time you are looking for a liberty item or have one to sell, try our site first. It's managed by Laurent Ghesquiere, club member.

-- Brian Snyder, Vice President & Webmaster
http://www.statueoflibertyclub.com

A club for collectors, lovers and everyone passionately fond of the Statue of Liberty.

Statue of Liberty Set To Reopen -- In Part

Visitors will be able to enter the base of the Statue of Liberty again on August 3, but they'll need a reservation, and they won't be able to go where they'd probably like to -- THE CROWN.

"Safety of our citizens and preservation of the statue are our main goals," said Interior Secretary Gale Norton, who called the statue "an attractive terrorist target."

They'll be able to see the interior of the statue through the pedestal's new glass ceiling. Liberty Island, the statue's home, reopened three months after 9/11. Visitors are screened by metal detectors before they board ferries to the island. Visits are down at least 40%. Tourism analysts agree that's largely because people want to go inside the statue.

THE STATUE OF LIBERTY CLUB. The Statue of Liberty Collectors' Club was founded by Iris November. Its members are enthusiasts of the statue, and most collect memorabilia and artifacts related to its history. In September and October 2004, club members traveled to Paris and Colmar, France, to commemorate the 100th anniversary of the death of Auguste Bartholdi, the man who sculpted Liberty.

THE PEDESTAL REOPENS.
The statue's pedestal was reopened for public visitation in a Liberty Island ceremony on August 3, 2004. The event was presided over by Secretary of the Interior Gale Norton; other participants included park superintendent Cynthia Garrett, Statue of Liberty Foundation president Stephen A. Briganti, Gov. George Pataki of New York, and Mayor Michael Bloomberg of New York City. Visitors may now go to the top of the pedestal and look through the newly installed glass ceiling to see the inside of the colossus above. (National Park Service.)

INDEX

American Committee, 42, 43, 44, 48, 49, 50, 57, 60
American Independence, 10, 21, 50, 116
American Museum of Immigration, 109, *110*, 113, *115*
Anniversaries, 46, *87-91*, 93, 97, *108-109*
Architecture, 43-45
Army (U.S.), 16-19, 40, 70, 71, *72*, 76, *100*, *110*
Aronson, Rudolph, 49
Arrival, *53*, *54*, *55*
Bartholdi, Auguste, 11, *14*, 16-22, 24-26, 28, 30, 32, 37, 39, 41, 50, 51, 60, 63, 66, 74, 75, 100, 121, 126
Bartholdi, Charlotte, *30*
Bartholdi Museum, 20
Bedloe's Island, *22*, 39, 40, 54-57, 58-60, 62, 68
Black Tom explosion, 67, 76
Borie, Victor, 24
Bozérian, Jean-François, 24
Briganti, Stephen, 126
Brodie, William, 46, 47
Butler, Richard, 42, 48
Camp, Charles, 46
Camp, Oswald Edward, 46, 85, 91, 92
Castle Garden (Castle Clinton), *72*
Cartoons, 48, 92
Celebrities, 49, *94*, *105*, *117*
Ceremonies, *23*, 25, *34*, 38, 47, 48, 60-62, 77, *86-91*, 93, 97, *102*, *108*, *109*
Chain and Shackle, 19, 83

Civil War, 9, 40, 52
Cleveland, Grover, 60, 61, *62*
Coins, 9, *12*, *13*, 14
Colossus of Rhodes (Helios), 16
Concession, 79
Construction, 27, 28, 29, 30, 32, 33, *34*, *35*, *36*, *37*, 46, 47, 52, 57-59
Coolidge, Calvin, 78
Copper, 25, 26, 28, 96, 118, 119, 120, 121
Cornerstone, 46, 47
Crown (diadem), 19, *94*, 98, *100*, *101*
Declaration of Independence, 116
Dedication, 60-62
DeLeo, Charles, *123*
Democracy, 10, 15, 21, 122
DePew, Chauncey Mitchell, 42, 60
DiPietro, Vincent, 123
Documents, *21*, *24*, *25*, *38*, 48, 62, 60
Dress, *37*, *84*, *110*
Drexel, Joseph, 48, 53
Egypt, 16-20, 41, 52
Egypt Carrying the Light to Asia, 16, *17*, *18*, 20
Eiffel, Gustave, 26, *33*, *34*
Eisenhower, Dwight, 110
Elevator, 69, *105*
Ellis Island, *72*, 86, *124*
Engineering, 26, 33, *34*, 47, 50, 52
Evarts, William Maxwell, 42, 48, 60

Ferries, 68, 86
Fort Wood, 40, 47, *70*, *71*, *72*, *80*, 98, *114*
Foster, Newell H., *107*
Foundation, *47*, 59
France, 9, 10-14, 15, 20-21, 23-28, 30-33, *34-38*, 50, 53-55, 60, 62, 93, *100*, 126, *102*
Franco-American Union, *23*, 24, 25, 38, 53, 60
Franco-Prussian War, 15, 50
French Navy, 53-55
Fund-raising, 23, 24, 25, *31*, *32*, 42, 48, 49, 50, 57, 74, 117, 126
Gaget, Gauthier & Company, 24, 27, 28
Goddess of Democracy, *122*
Goddess of Liberty, 12, *13*, 16, 63, 93, 122
Golden Jubilee, 46, *86-91*
Gounod, Charles, 25
Grable, Betty, *94*
Granite, 40, 44, 45
Hayes, Rutherford B., 22
Head, *30*, *31*, *36*, *94*
Height, 16, 44
Hill family, 79
Hunt, Richard Morris, 42, 43, 44, 45, 52
Iacocca, Lee, *117*
Ickes, Harold, *91*
Immigration, 64, *72*, *73*, *74*, 75, *110*, *115*
Internal structure, 33, *35*, 96
Isère, *53*, *54*, *55*
Isma'il Pasha, 16
Jay, John, 42

127

King, David H., Jr., 52, 59
Laboulaye, Edouard de, *10, 11-13*, 15, 19, 22, 23-25, 38, 63
Lafayette, Marquis de, 21
LaGuardia, Fiorello, *91*
Lazarus, Emma, *73, 74*
Lefaivre, W. Albert, 60
Lesseps, Viscount de, 38, 53, 60
Lockett, Samuel, 52
Liberty (Libertas), 12, 13, 16, 19, 63, 93, 122
Liberty Bell inscription, *15*
Liberty Island, 62, *109*
Lighthouse, 18, 68
Lighting, *100, 101*
Lincoln, Abraham, 9
Lion of Belfort, 14, *50*
Louis-Noël, Hubert, 75
Macé, Jean, 24
McLaughlin, James, *71, 72*
Madison Square Park, 49
Maps, 20, 39
Martin, Henri, 24
Masonic influence, *21, 46, 47*
Measurements, *67*
Meredith, Burgess, *105*
Miss Liberty, 105
Models (*maquettes*), 16-19, 30, 100
Monarchy, 10, 11, 15, 21
Monduit, Honoré, 24, *27*
Monuments, *16, 50, 65*
Moran, Edward, 61
Morgan, Edwin Denison, 42
Morton, Levi Parsons, 34, 38
Morton, Rogers, *115*
Napoléon III, 10, *15*
National monument, 78
National Park Service, 46, 80, 81, 85, 92, 99, 100, 105-107
New York Harbor, 16, 20, 22, 42, 50, 53-56, 82, 86, *104, 111*
Nimbus, 16, 85, *94-95*
Nixon, Richard M., 110, *115*
Norwegian copper, 25
November, Iris, 126
Origins, 9-22, 100
Palmer, George A., 80, 81,

100
Paris Universal Exposition, *31*
Pedestal, *34, 41, 42, 43, 44,45*, 46, 47, 49, 51, 52, *57*, 69, 95, *114, 125, 126*
Philadelphia, 29, 50
Phrygian bonnet, *13*
Piaf, Edith, *105*
Pickering, Simeon Horace, *105*
Pitkin, Thomas M., 110
Poem ("The New Colossus"), *74*
Presentation, 38, 63
Presidents, 9, 21, 22, 60, 61, 62, 78, 89-91,110, *115, 117,* 118
Pulitzer, Joseph, *57*, 115
Radio broadcasts, *91*, 105
Reagan, Ronald, *117*, 118
Repoussé technique, 26, 28
Restoration, 94, 95, *117, 118-122*
Roman influence, 12, 13, 84
Roosevelt, Franklin Delano, *89-91*
Roosevelt, Theodore Sr., 42
Russell, Lillian, 49
Sabotage, 67, 76
Sculpture, *11*, 14, *16-20*, 21, 50, 65, *74, 75, 100*, 122
Seaton, Fred A., *108, 109*
September 11th Attacks, *124*, 125
Sérurier, Count, 24
Sherman, William T., *22*, 40
Ships, *53-55*, 88, 89, *112*
Simonin, Louis-Laurent, 24
Slavery, 9, 12, 13, 83
Smith, Francis Hopkinson, 47
Spaulding, Henry F., 48
Stairs, *79*, 95, *96*
Statue of Liberty Club, *126*
Statue of Liberty–Ellis Island Foundation, 125
Stokes, Anson Phelps, 42
Stone, Charles P., 47, *52*, 53, 59
Symbolism, 9, 12, 13, 15, 16, 64, 73-77, 83, 84, 122

Suez monument, 16-20
Tablet, *32*, 62, 85, *116*
Terrorism, *124, 125*
Tone, Franchot, *105*
Torch and Flame, 19, *29, 50*, 67, 68, 84, *91, 123*
Tourism, 67, 68, 69, 79, 81, 86, 94, 98, 99, *102-107*
Union League Club, 42, 60
Unveiling ceremony, *61*, 62
Veterans of Foreign Wars (Ladies Auxiliary), 87, 97
Viollet-le-Duc, Eugène, 24, 26, 33, *121*
Waddington, William, 24
Washington, George, 21
Wingate, John, 105
Witt, Cornélis de, 24
Wolowski, Louis, 24
The World (*newspaper*), 57
World Trade Center, 123, *124*
World War I, *77*
World War II, 99, *100*